First Ladies

Laura Bush

by Sally Lee

Consulting Editor: Gail Saunders-Smith, PhD

Consultant: Carl Sferrazza Anthony, Historian
National First Ladies' Library
Canton, Ohio

CAPSTONE PRESS
a capstone imprint

Pebble Plus is published by Capstone Press,
151 Good Counsel Drive, P.O. Box 669, Mankato, Minnesota 56002.
www.capstonepub.com

Books published by Capstone Press are manufactured with paper
containing at least 10 percent post-consumer waste.

Library of Congress Cataloging-in-Publication Data
Lee, Sally.
  Laura Bush / by Sally Lee.
    p. cm.—(Pebble plus. First ladies)
  Includes bibliographical references and index.
  Summary: "Simple text and photographs describe the life of Laura Bush"—Provided by publisher.
  ISBN 978-1-4296-5325-1 (library binding)
  1. Bush, Laura Welch, 1946—Juvenile literature. 2. Presidents' spouses—United States--Biography—Juvenile
literature. 3. Teachers—Texas—Biography—Juvenile literature. 4. Librarians—Texas—Biography—Juvenile literature.
I. Title. II. Series.
  E904.B87L44 2011
  973.931092—dc22   2010024907

Editorial Credits

Erika L. Shores, editor; Ashlee Suker, designer; Svetlana Zhurkin, media researcher;
    Laura Manthe, production specialist

Photo Credits

AP Photo/Harry Cabluck, 5
Corbis/Sygma/David Woo, 12–13
George Bush Presidential Library, 11
Getty Images/Pool/Alyssa Cwanger, 17; Stefan Zaklin, 15
Landov/UPI/Lio Mizrahi, 6–7
Newscom/AFP/Saul Loeb, 18–19; UPI/Michael Bush, 1, 21
Shutterstock/Alaettin Yildirim, 5, 7, 9 (caption plate); antoninaart, cover (left), 1, 4–5, 10–11, 22–23, 24 (pattern);
    Gemenacom, 5, 11 (frame); vpix, cover (right)
Wikipedia/Spencerjc1, 9

Note to Parents and Teachers

The First Ladies series supports national history standards related to people and culture.
This book describes and illustrates the life of Laura Bush. The images support early readers
in understanding the text. The repetition of words and phrases helps early readers learn new
words. This book also introduces early readers to subject-specific vocabulary words, which are
defined in the Glossary section. Early readers may need assistance to read some words and to
use the Table of Contents, Glossary, Read More, Internet Sites, and Index sections of the book.

Printed in the United States of America in North Mankato, Minnesota.
092010
005933CGS11

Table of Contents

Early Years 4

Family Life. 10

First Lady 14

Glossary 22

Read More 23

Internet Sites. 23

Index 24

Early Years

Laura Bush wants every child
to know how to read.
The future librarian and
first lady was born in Midland,
Texas, on November 4, 1946.
She was Harold and Jenna
Welch's only child.

born in
Texas

1946

Laura and her mother,
Jenna Welch, in 2000

Laura was a quiet but friendly
girl who loved books.
She knew by second grade
that she wanted to
be a teacher.

born in
Texas

1946

As first lady, Laura showed her love of teaching by visiting schools.

In 1964 Laura attended college to become a teacher. She taught school for several years. Then her love of books led her back to college to become a librarian.

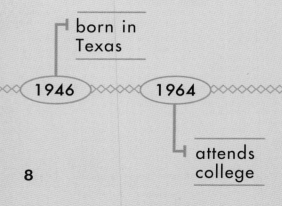

born in
Texas

1946   1964

attends
college

Laura graduated from Southern Methodist University in 1968.

Family Life

Laura married George W. Bush
in 1977. They had twin daughters.
George wanted to run for
public office. At first, Laura was
too shy to give speeches for him.

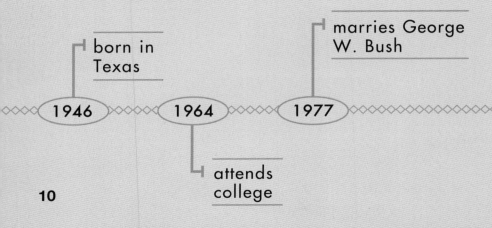

marries George
W. Bush

born in
Texas

1946 1964 1977

attends
college

In 1995 George became governor of Texas.

Laura was the state's first lady. She encouraged families to read more. She started the Texas Book Festival to raise money for libraries.

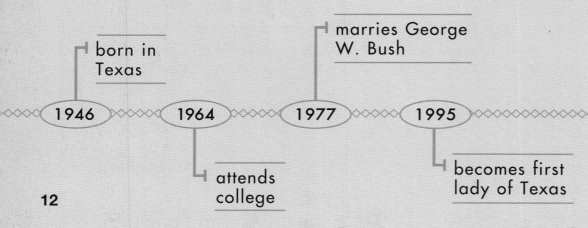

marries George W. Bush

born in Texas

1946   1964   1977   1995

attends college

becomes first lady of Texas

First Lady

George became president
of the United States in 2001.
As first lady, Laura worked to
improve education for young
children. She spoke out for better
pay and training for teachers.

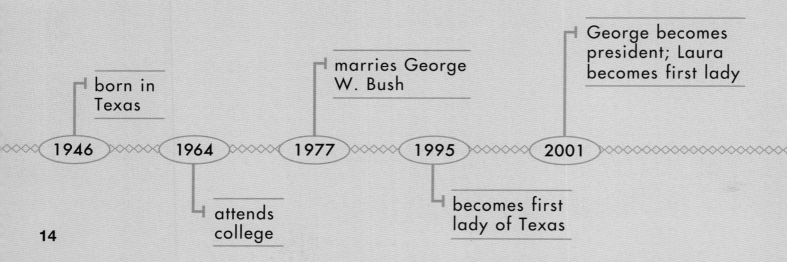

born in
Texas

marries George
W. Bush

George becomes
president; Laura
becomes first lady

1946   1964   1977   1995   2001

attends
college

becomes first
lady of Texas

On September 11, 2001, terrorists attacked the United States. Laura comforted those who were sad and afraid. She told children they were safe and loved. She visited the families of victims.

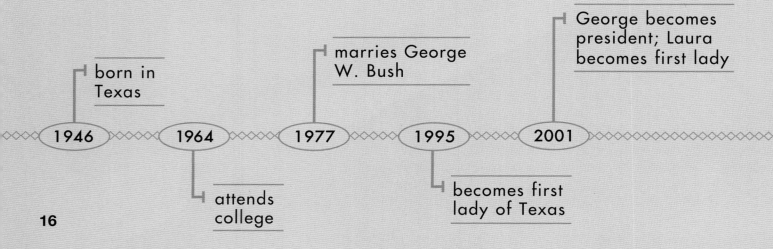

born in Texas

marries George W. Bush

George becomes president; Laura becomes first lady

1946   1964   1977   1995   2001

attends college

becomes first lady of Texas

Laura cared about people everywhere. She was against governments that refused human rights to their people. She helped get schools for girls and job training for women in Afghanistan.

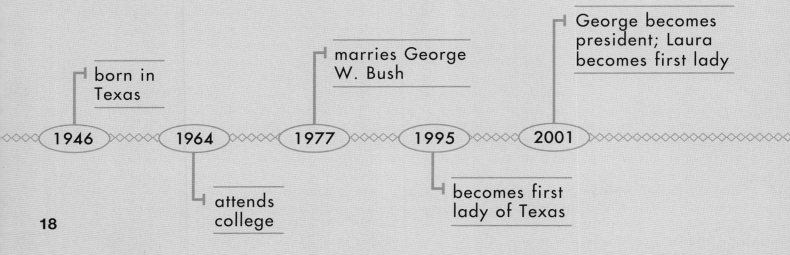

born in Texas

1946

marries George W. Bush

1977

George becomes president; Laura becomes first lady

2001

1964

attends college

1995

becomes first lady of Texas

In 2009 George and Laura
moved back to Texas.
Laura will be remembered
for bringing the joy of reading
to people of all ages.

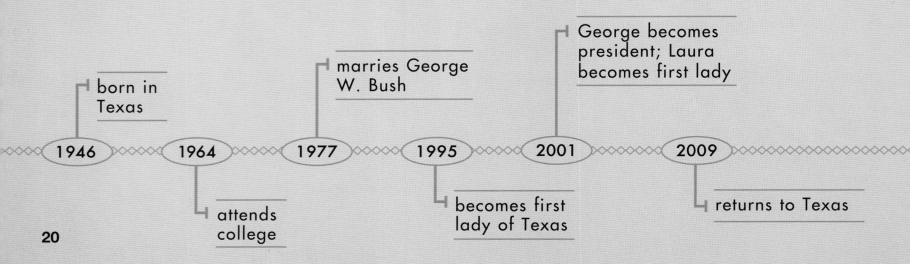

born in
Texas

1946

attends
college

1964

marries George
W. Bush

1977

becomes first
lady of Texas

1995

George becomes
president; Laura
becomes first lady

2001

returns to Texas

2009

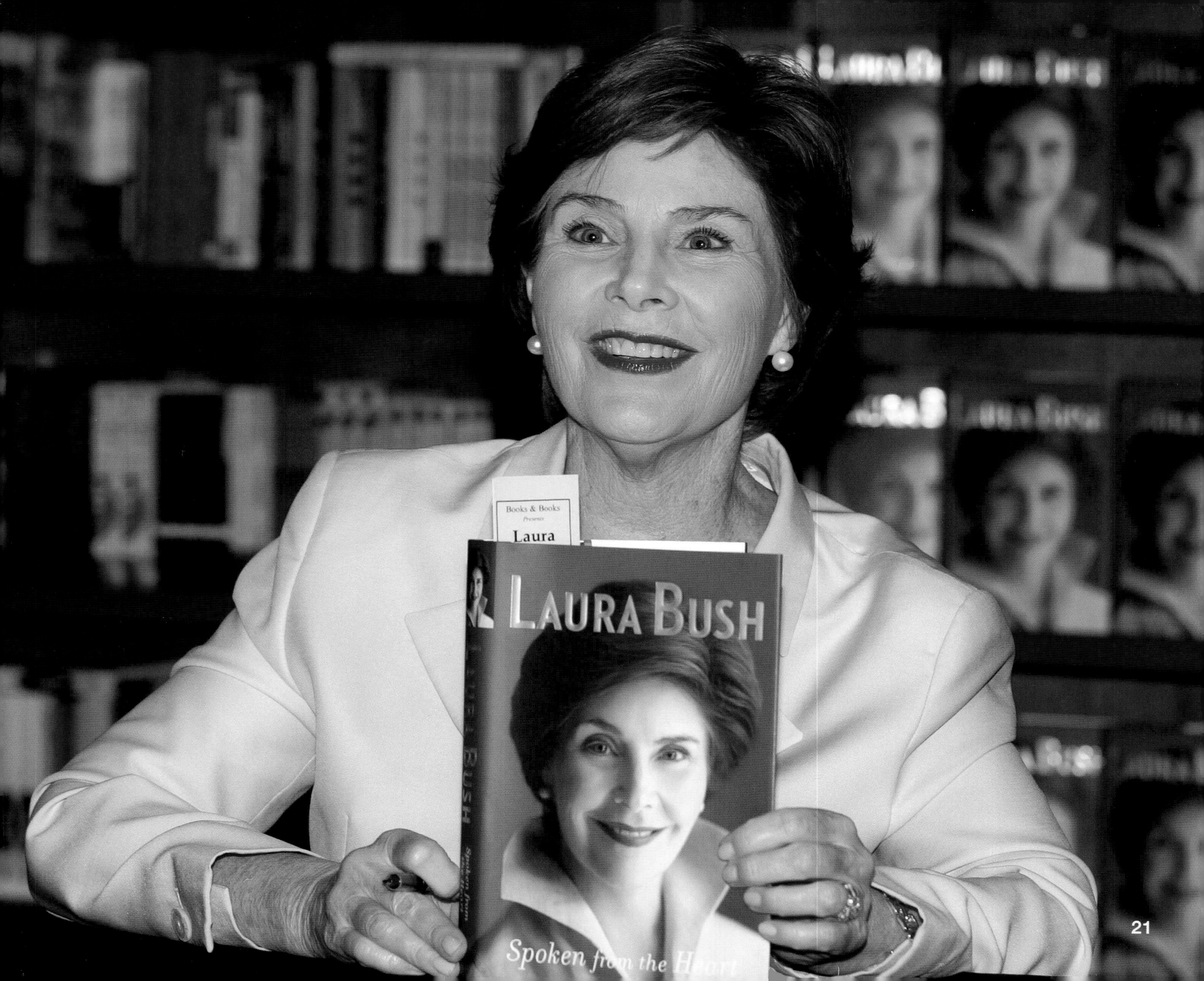
Books & Books
Presents
Laura
LAURA BUSH
BUSH

Glossary

college—school that comes after high school

encourage—to urge someone to do something

human rights—the basic freedoms that all people deserve to have

public office—a job serving the people or government; a person who runs for public office is voted on by the people

terrorist—a person who uses harmful acts and fear to get what they want

victim—someone who is hurt or killed by a person, group, or event

Read more

Bush, Laura and Jenna Bush. *Read All About It!* New York: Harper Collins Publishers, 2008.

Mara, Wil. *Laura Bush.* Rookie Biographies. New York: Children's Press, 2003.

Our White House: Looking In, Looking Out. Cambridge, Mass.: Candlewick Press, 2008.

Internet Sites

FactHound offers a safe, fun way to find Internet sites related to this book. All of the sites on FactHound have been researched by our staff.

Here's all you do:

Visit *www.facthound.com*

Type in this code: 9781429653251

Super-cool stuff! Check out projects, games and lots more at www.capstonekids.com

Index

Afghanistan, 18
birth, 4
Bush, George W., 10, 12, 14, 20
college, 8
daughters, 10
first lady, 4, 12, 14
human rights, 18

librarian, 4, 8
parents, 4
reading, 4, 12, 20
September 11
   terrorist attacks, 16
teacher, 6, 8
Texas Book Festival, 12

Word Count: 257
Grade: 1
Early-Intervention Level: 20